Eddie and Ellie's Opposites
At the Farm

Rebecca Rissman

Raintree

Raintree is an imprint of Capstone Global Library Limited, a company incorporated in England and Wales having its registered office at 7 Pilgrim Street, London, EC4V 6LB – Registered company number: 6695582

www.raintreepublishers.co.uk
myorders@raintreepublishers.co.uk

Text © Capstone Global Library Limited 2014
First published in hardback in 2014
Paperback edition first published in 2015
The moral rights of the proprietor have been asserted.

Edited by Rebecca Rissman, Daniel Nunn, and Catherine Veitch
Designed by Jo Hinton-Malivoire
Original illustrations © Capstone Global Library Ltd 2013
Illustrations by Steve Walker
Picture research by Ruth Blair
Production by Sophia Argyris
Originated by Capstone Global Library Ltd
Printed and bound in China by Leo Paper
Products Ltd

ISBN 978 1 406 26313 8 (hardback)
17 16 15 14 13
10 9 8 7 6 5 4 3 2 1

ISBN 978 1 406 26318 3 (paperback)
18 17 16 15 14
10 9 8 7 6 5 4 3 2 1

British Library Cataloguing in Publication Data
A full catalogue record for this book is available from the British Library.

Acknowledgements
We would like to thank the following for permission to reproduce photographs: Shutterstock pp. 7t (© chuyu), 7b (© Alex Staroseltsev), 8 (© Sandra Cunningham), 9l (© Eric Gevaert), 9r (© Iakov Filimonov), 10 (© Tyler Olson), 11 (© Keith Publicover), 12 (© mkm3), 13 (© bayberry), 14 (© Le Do), 15 (© i4lcocl2), 16 (© Mazzzur), 17 (© Igor Borodin), 18 (© pirita), 19 (© Arno van Dulmen), 20 (© AISPIX by Image Source), 21 (© Brocreative), 22 (© yuriy kulik, © Vaclav Mach), 23l (© Tony Campbell), 23r (© wdeon).

Cover photograph of geese reproduced with permission of Shutterstock (© Regien Paassen).

Every effort has been made to contact copyright holders of any material reproduced in this book. Any omissions will be rectified in subsequent printings if notice is given to the publisher.

Contents

Meet Eddie and Ellie

This is Ellie the Elephant.

This is her friend, Eddie the Elephant.

Ellie and Eddie don't always agree.

Opposites

Eddie and Ellie almost always like opposite things!

Opposites are completely different from each other.

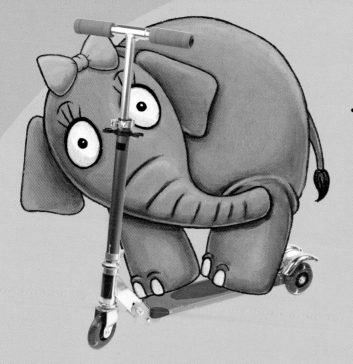

This morning Ellie woke up bright and **EARLY**.

But Eddie slept in and woke up **LATE**.

A visit to a farm

This afternoon, Eddie and Ellie are going to visit a farm.

Some farms raise animals. Some farms grow crops. Some farms do both!

Farmers work on farms.

Dirty and clean

Ellie likes dirty animals at the farm.
This pig is **DIRTY**.

Eddie likes clean animals at the farm.
These ducks are **CLEAN**.

Big and small

Ellie likes to look at big animals at the farm.

Bulls are **BIG**.

Eddie likes to look at small animals at the farm. Rabbits are **SMALL**.

Quiet and loud

Ellie likes quiet jobs at the farm.

Picking weeds is a **QUIET** job.

Eddie likes loud jobs at the farm. Driving the tractor is a **LOUD** job.

Tall and short

Ellie likes tall plants at the farm.
Apple trees are **TALL**.

Eddie likes short plants at the farm. Strawberry plants are **SHORT**.

Fast and slow

Ellie likes animals that are fast.

Horses run *FAST.*

Eddie likes animals that are slow.

Cows are
SLOW.

Young and old

Ellie likes young farmers.
This farmer is **YOUNG**.

Eddie likes old farmers.
This farmer is **OLD**.

Can you work it out?

Ellie likes farm work that is **HARD**.

22

Do you think Eddie likes work that is **HARD** or **EASY?**

Opposites quiz

Do you know the opposites
for these words?

bright   **deep**   **long**

Answers

Answers to quiz

The opposite of bright is dull.
The opposite of deep is shallow.
The opposite of long is short.

Answer to question on page 23
Eddie likes farm work that is easy.

24